Reader's Guide to Wealth
The Best Books on Personal Finance

Table of Contents

Chapter 1. Introduction

Navigating the world of personal finance can often feel like exploring a labyrinth, full of confusing twists and turns. Thankfully, a multitude of books have been crafted by financial gurus worldwide, each providing unique maps to choose your path to financial stability and growth. Our comprehensive Special Report, 'Reader's Guide to Wealth: The Best Books on Personal Finance,' serves as the ultimate compass, guiding you through this complex domain. Within the pages of this report, you will uncover summaries of the best titles, reviews that illuminate their perspectives, and the key takeaways that can enhance your financial understanding. This vibrant journey of financial literacy awaits you, promising to empower you towards the prosperous future you deserve. Get ready to turn the pages towards financial freedom. Your wealth, much like your potential, awaits. Let's dive into this riveting voyage of discovery, prosperity, and financial success together.

Chapter 2. Understanding the Basics of Personal Finance

The labyrinthine realm of personal finance may initially seem daunting. However, understanding its basic tenets can demystify the path to financial fitness.

2.1. The Core Financial Principles

The universal principles of personal finance are relatable across all income levels, ages, and financial statuses. Let us unravel these principles:

1. Spend Less Than You Earn: It may seem like a no-brainer, but how often do we find ourselves trapped in a cycle of poor spending habits? Financial growth is virtually impossible if you habitually spend more than your earnings.

2. Invest Early and Regularly: The power of compound interest is most effective when utilized over long periods. Starting your investment journey at a young age can contribute significantly to wealth accumulation.

3. The Power of Diversification: A diversified financial portfolio spreads risks across various assets. This strategy protects one's finances from market volatility.

4. Emergency Fund: An unforeseen financial emergency can derail the strongest financial plan. An emergency fund, preferably around six months of living expenses, acts as a safety net during times of crises.

Following these principles, your financial health can vastly improve, thus enabling you to navigate financial turns with increased confidence.

2.2. The Importance of Budgeting

An organized budget is the cornerstone of strong personal finance. It records income, tracks spending, and assigns money to different financial goals. Budgeting illuminates the path to financial success by requiring deliberate thought about spending and saving. A simple monthly budget could break down as:

- 50% of income for necessities (rent, utilities, groceries)
- 30% of income for wants (dining, entertainment)
- 20% of income for savings and debt repayment

These percentages may differ based on personal circumstances, but it's essential to maintain a balance between these components for a healthy financial life.

2.3. Understanding the Concept of Debt

The role of debt in personal finance is often misconstrued. When used responsibly, debt aids our financial growth, enabling us to invest in higher education and real estate. However, mismanagement of debt can lead to challenges like bankruptcy and mental health issues.

Key components of responsible debt management include understanding the terms of the debt, scrutinizing interest rates, maintaining a consistent payment schedule, and maintaining a low debt-to-income ratio.

2.4. Investments and their role

Investing transforms your saved money into an active participant in wealth-building. It plays a critical part in the accumulation of wealth and achieving financial goals. Investments come in several forms - stocks, bonds, mutual funds, real estate, and more.

Investing is more than playing the stock market. It refers to a long-term commitment to let your money grow over time. Every investment carries some risk, but strategic investing and diversification of your investment portfolio can minimize this exposure.

2.5. Financial Planning for Retirement

Retirement planning guarantees a steady income post-retirement. Start your retirement savings as early as possible to reap the benefits of compound interest. Several retirement savings vehicles are available, like 401(k), IRA, Roth IRA, annuities, and more.

The financial need at retirement must consider the effect of inflation, the lifespan, and health issues. Thus, a substantial nest egg accumulated over your working years is essential for a comfortable retirement.

2.6. Importance of Insurance

Insurance safeguards against financial loss and offers protection for your finances, health, life, and possessions. Be it health insurance, term life insurance, homeowner's insurance, or auto insurance; each serves as a form of financial backstop to a different kind of risk, maintaining stability amid uncertainties.

2.7. Tax Planning

Effective tax planning can save substantial amounts and contribute to wealth building. Careful tax planning comprises utilizing tax credits, deductions, understanding tax brackets, and aligning one's financial activities, resulting in minimized tax liabilities.

2.8. Estate Planning

Estate planning ensures your assets get distributed as per your wishes posthumously. It includes wills, trusts, power of attorney, and healthcare proxies. While death is an uncomfortable topic, an estate plan saves families from financial hardship and legal limbo during trying times.

Understanding the basics of personal finance is the first step in your journey to financial independence. In grasping these principles, you equip yourself with the knowledge to make informed decisions, kickstart your financial plan, and unlock the doors to your prosperous future.

Chapter 3. Setting Goals for Financial Success

When it comes to financial success, one cannot understress the importance of setting clear, measurable, and attainable goals. While luck can occasionally play a role, wealth is more frequently the result of sound financial planning, strict strategy implementation, and discipline. This chapter aims to guide you in defining your financial goals and creating paths that will lead you to financial success.

3.1. Defining Your Financial Goals

Think of your financial goals as the destinations on your personal journey towards financial success. These goals can vary widely depending on factors such as age, salary, lifestyle, family structure, among other unique personal factors. For some, it may mean becoming debt-free, for others, it might be purchasing a house, perhaps retiring comfortably is your aim.

In order to give shape to your goals, start by asking yourself the following questions:

- What would I like to achieve financially in the next few years?
- Where do I envision myself financially in a decade?
- What are my ultimate financial aspirations?

Use the answers to these questions to make a list of short-term (1-3 years), mid-term (3-5 years), and long-term goals (10+ years). Each of these classifications serve a purpose within your overarching financial plan and their reach is defined by the time taken to achieve them. While short-term goals can cater to immediate financial needs, long-term goals accommodate for more significant milestones like retirement or purchasing property.

3.2. Quantifying Your Goals

After defining what your goals are, the next step involves quantifying them. Put down the required amount for each of your goals, alongside their timelines. This practice not only makes your goals more achievable but also gives you insight into prioritizing them. For instance, if saving for your child's college education is a long-term goal, determine the amount you foresee needing, considering inflation and rising tuition costs.

Similarly, if buying a home is a mid-term goal, determine the down payment you need to save for. This exercise will help you realize the financial commitment behind each goal and factor them in your budgeting and investment strategies.

3.3. Creating a Budget

Crafting a budget is an integral step in reaching your financial goals. It brings clarity to your current financial status, enabling you to figure out how much you can set aside towards each goal. Here is a simplified way to draw up a budget:

1. List your income sources.
2. Deduct your fixed expenses like rent, mortgage, utilities, and other bills.
3. Calculate your variable expenses, including groceries, entertainment, and discretionary spending.
4. Deduct your fixed and variable expenses from your income to determine your possible savings.

Apply the 50/30/20 rule to your spending. Allocate 50% of your income to needs, 30% to wants, and 20% to saving and paying off debts. This simple yet effective rule allows for financial balance and goal-setting.

3.4. Implementing a Saving and Investing Strategy

Any financial plan's efficacy is tested by how well you save and invest. Start by creating an emergency fund to cover six months to a year of living expenses, securing you against unexpected financial setbacks. Once your emergency buffer is ready, distribute the rest of your savings towards your goals as per their priority and timeline.

To speed up the process, consider investing a part of your savings. However, it's vital to understand that investing carries risk, and the key is to balance risk and reward by diversifying your investments. Consider different asset allocations such as equities, bonds, real estate, amongst others, depending on your risk tolerance, age, and financial goals. Always invest with a clear understanding of your chosen investment products.

3.5. Monitoring and Revising Your Goals

Once your goals are defined, quantified, and set in motion, the next essential step is monitoring and revising them periodically. Your income, expenses, personal situation, or market conditions may change over time, affecting your ability to reach your goals. Regularly evaluating your financial plan in response to these changes can help you stay on track.

In conclusion, setting goals is fundamental to achieving financial success. It provides direction, quantifies milestones, and encourages discipline. By painting a picture of where you want to go, setting goals highlights the steps needed to get there. Remember, always define, quantify, strategize, monitor, and, if necessary, revise your goals. Financial success isn't accomplished overnight; it's the journey and the discipline that it instills, which ultimately leads to wealth accumulation.

Chapter 4. Budget Mastery: Moving from Theory to Practice

Finance gurus instruct that mastering one's budget is one of the premier steps in the journey towards fiscal stability, and they aren't wrong. The understanding begins with a clear overview of your income and spending, identifying problem areas, setting feasible financial goals, and a steady commitment to the budgeting process. Let's demystify the concept, transitioning from budgeting theories into tangible practice.

4.1. Theoretical Foundations

First, let's begin by understanding the theory underlying the budgeting process. A budget, in essence, is a plan for your money. It's a proactive approach towards money management instead of a mere reactive response to emergencies. The concept of budgeting can be rooted in two main theories:

- Modern Money Management Theory: Proposes the importance of tailoring budgeting to individual needs, and it revolves around adapting existing money management strategies to singular financial circumstances.

- Traditional Financial Planning Theory: Advocates a more disciplined approach, emphasizing saving, investing, and creating strict boundaries for different spending categories.

While shifting to the practical end of this endeavor, it's ideal to take both theoretical perspectives into account. By marrying custom-tailored financial tactics with disciplined planning, you can create a robust budget that accurately reflects and aids your monetary goals.

4.2. Income and Spending Assessment

Now, let us transition into pragmatic budgeting. Start by analyzing your income and spending.

Both your primary sources of income (such as regular salary) and secondary income (from side jobs or investments) should be clearly enumerated and summed up. Then, break down your expenses into two categories - fixed and variable.

Include costs like rent, loan repayments, bills that remain constant each month in fixed expenditures. Conversely, variable expenses include groceries, entertainment, eating out, which tend to fluctuate. This comprehensive assessment will provide a bird's eye view of your financial state, the first stride towards budget mastery.

4.3. Identifying Financial Goals

Once you've got your revenue and expenses laid down clearly, it's time to identify your financial goals. They can be short-term, such as buying a new gadget, mid-term like planning a vacation, or long-term—they may include purchasing a home or retirement planning.

Assign each goal an estimated cost and a target completion date. This makes your goals more tangible and provides a checklist to measure your financial progress against.

4.4. Creating Your Budget

With your financial landscape and goals clearly defined, it's time to create your budget. There are several methodologies you can implement -

- Zero-Based Budgeting assigns every dollar of income to an expense category until you're left with zero. It ensures every penny is accounted for.

- The 50/30/20 Rule is more lenient; it suggests dividing your income into necessities (50%), wants (30%), and savings (20%).

Choose what aligns with your financial temperament.

4.5. Implementation and Review

Once you've plotted out your budget, dedicate yourself to its implementation. You might stumble initially, experiencing discrepancies between the anticipated and actual expenditure. Don't let this discourage you. Review your budget regularly, adjusting when necessary.

With your budget in place, you're ideally positioned to control your financing, realize your financial goals, and grow your wealth. Budget mastery is a constantly evolving process, reflecting changes in your income, lifestyle, and goals. Commitment to it is indeed the beginning of the practical application of personal finance theory. Stick with this journey to discover the power and possibility that a well-crafted budget can unlock.

Chapter 5. Saving Smart: The Road to Wealth Accumulation

Starting on the journey of wealth accumulation begins with the understanding and implementation of savings. A solid savings plan is the cornerstone of any strong personal financial strategy, a safety net, and a first step towards investment. However, being 'smart' at saving requires discipline, knowledge, and a sound strategy.

5.1. The Fundamentals of Smart Saving

Smart saving begins with setting up a clear and attainable financial goal. These goals could range from general - saving for retirement, to specific – buying a house within five years. The goal could also revolve around short-term objectives, long-term milestones, or an emergency fund.

Once the goal has been set, calculating the amount to save involves understanding your income and expenses. Keep track of your cash inflows and outflows, note your necessities, and the portion that can be shaved off for savings. A general rule of thumb is to save at least 20% of your income. However, this ratio can be adjusted based on individual circumstances and aspirations.

5.2. Implementing the 50/30/20 Rule

A common strategy amongst effective savers is following the 50/30/20 rule. This rule suggests that 50% of your income should go to necessities (like food, rent, and bills), 30% to lifestyle choices (like entertainment and dining out), and the remaining 20% to savings.

The power of this rule lies in its simplicity and adaptability, catering to different income brackets while still encouraging saving. Adhering to this guideline can provide a balanced approach to spending and saving, ensuring necessary expenses are covered while securing a financial future.

5.3. Automating Your Savings

One of the best ways to ensure consistent saving is to automate it. Many banking services offer the option to automatically transfer a portion of your income to your savings or investment accounts. This method removes the chance of forgetfulness or temptation to spend.

This practice reinforces the concept of "paying yourself first." Before spending on monthly expenses and luxury items, put aside a portion of your income for savings. Over time, this method can lead to significant accumulation of wealth.

5.4. The Importance of an Emergency Fund

An emergency fund acts as a financial buffer, protecting you from unforeseen circumstances such as job loss, medical emergencies or sudden large expenses. The recommended amount is usually three to six months' worth of living expenses. This fund should be easily accessible, but separate from your regular transaction account to avoid the temptation to dip into it for daily expenses.

5.5. Understanding the Power of Compound Interest

Albert Einstein reportedly said, "Compound interest is the eighth wonder of the world. He who understands it, earns it; he who doesn't, pays it."

Compounding is a powerful financial tool that amplifies your savings growth by earning interest on the interest already earned. If you start early, even with a relatively small amount, it can result in substantial growth over time due to the snowball effect of compound interest.

For example, if you begin with $1000 as principal and earn an annual interest of 5%, you will have $1050 at the end of year one. During the second year, interest is calculated on the $1050, rather than the original $1000, resulting in a total of $1102.50. As the years go by, this increase multiplies.

5.6. Choosing the Right Savings Accounts

A critical aspect of smart saving is placing your money in a savings account with a competitive interest rate. Different savings accounts come with different interest rates, perks, and penalties for withdrawal which can significantly influence your savings growth. Research and compare accounts to find one that will maximize your wealth accumulation.

5.7. Diversifying Your Savings

Just as putting all your eggs in one basket isn't a smart move, putting all your savings in one place may not be the best approach to wealth accumulation. Diversification of savings refers to spreading your savings across different financial instruments like savings accounts, fixed deposits, bonds, and mutual funds. This method can safeguard against risk while potentially increasing your returns.

5.8. Reviewing and Adjusting Your Plan

Saving strategies are not static. They must be reviewed and adjusted regularly, determined by changes in income, living circumstances, financial goals, and macroeconomic factors. Regular check-ins will keep your savings plan attuned to your current financial reality and future aspirations.

Having embarked on this extensive discussion of smart saving, we hope to have not only provided an understanding of the concept but a clear roadmap to commence your wealth accumulation journey. Savings, when done smartly, is a powerful tool that sets the foundation for a secure and prosperous future. With these guidelines, you are now equipped to embark on your path towards financial stability and growth. Happy saving!

Chapter 6. Unraveling the Mysteries of Investment

Every successful financial journey inevitably involves an essential component - investment. It is the cornerstone of wealth creation, a tool instrumental in converting today's earnings into tomorrow's wealth. However, understanding investment can often feel like unthreading an intricate knot. So, let's start unpacking this captivating world of investing.

6.1. The Fundamentals of Investment

Investment is, in essence, the process of allocating money or other resources with an expectation of earning a profit or a financial return. The resources so allocated, otherwise known as 'investments,' could take various forms, such as cash, property, bonds, or equities, among others.

Investments effectively facilitate the transformation of current income into future wealth, capitalizing on the key economic principles of compounding and time value of money. The strategic allocation of resources in promising avenues results in returns that, when reinvested, create a cumulative effect over time called compounding.

Investment avenues are classified broadly into two categories: debt and equity. Debt involves lending your money for a fixed return, while equity implies owning a part of an enterprise and thereby partaking in its growth and profitability.

6.2. Understanding the Risk-Reward Spectrum

One of the fundamental aspects to grasp in the investment domain is the risk-reward tradeoff. Higher risk investments such as equities (stocks) often come with the potential for higher returns, but also a greater chance of capital loss. Lower risk investments like bonds and certificates of deposit offer lower returns but provide more capital safety.

Considered on a risk-reward spectrum, at one end, you have low-risk, low-return options like government bonds and fixed deposits, while relatively high-risk, high-return options such as equities and real estate sit at the other end.

Understanding your risk tolerance - how much risk you can afford to take - and aligning it with your financial goals is crucial in selecting the appropriate mix of investments within your portfolio. This calibration is often based on factors such as age, income level, financial objectives, and personal comfort with risk.

6.3. Diversification and Asset Allocation

No discussion on investing is complete without addressing the concepts of diversification and asset allocation. These are essentially risk management strategies that aim to optimize returns by spreading investments across various asset classes and sectors.

Diversification involves owning a mix of assets that aren't correlated. The theory here is that if one asset underperforms, the losses incurred can be offset by other investments performing well. This practice, colloquially known as "not putting all your eggs in one basket," reduces portfolio risk and can result in smoother, more consistent returns over time.

Asset allocation furthers this concept by determining the optimal distribution of investments between varying asset classes. This typically depends on an individual's financial goals, investment time frame, and risk appetite.

6.4. The Art of Stock Picking

Stock picking involves analyzing and selecting individual stocks for investment. This process generally incorporates either a fundamental, technical, or quantitative approach, or often a blend of all three.

Fundamental analysis looks at a company's financials and industry position to assess its intrinsic value, while technical analysis uses statistical trends derived from trading activity, such as price movement and volume. Quantitative analysis employs sophisticated mathematical models to understand patterns and trends within the market.

While stock picking can reward investors with superior returns, it demands thorough knowledge, continuous market research, and a comprehensive understanding of the global economic landscape.

6.5. Role of Mutual Funds

For those less inclined to pick individual stocks, mutual funds offer a convenient, professionally managed way to participate in the financial markets. A mutual fund pools money from many investors to purchase a diversified portfolio of bonds, stocks, or other assets.

Mutual funds provide instant diversification, professional management, and are ideal for those who prefer a relatively hands-off approach to investing. They come in several varieties - Equity funds, Bond funds, Money Market funds, and Hybrid funds, each catering to different investment objectives and risk appetites.

Investing is a powerful tool, a trusty vehicle to ferry you to the shores of financial prosperity. Yet, like any journey, you will encounter challenging terrains of market volatility or the haze of economic uncertainty. Armed with the investing fundamentals mentioned here, you are positioned better to navigate these inevitable challenges. Remember, the art and science of investing is not merely about making money, but about paving the way for financial independence and creating the wealth needed to finance your dreams.

Chapter 7. Credit and Debt: The Double-Edged Sword

Understanding the fundamental dynamics around credit and debt is an essential part of personal financial literacy. These two components are intrinsic in almost all our monetary transactions, in one way or another, and mastering them paves the way towards a stable fiscal future.

7.1. Understanding Credit

Credit, in essence, is the trust that allows one party to provide money or resources to another party. In most cases, the lender expects to get this money back in the future, usually with interest. However, credit doesn't only involve money. It may also apply to goods and services or any other valuable item.

Banks, credit card companies, and other financial institutions assess your creditworthiness — or how likely you are to repay borrowed money — by checking your credit history and score. The better these numbers and records, the more likely you are to receive credit with favorable terms, such as lower interest rates.

7.2. Knowing Your Credit Score

Your credit score is a numeric expression of your creditworthiness, often ranging between 300 and 850 with the higher the score, the better. In the U.S., three major credit bureaus monitor and provide these scores: Equifax, Experian, and TransUnion.

Your credit score is calculated based on five primary factors: . Payment history – comprises 35% of your score; signifies reliability in paying debts on time. . Amounts owed – 30%; signals responsible handling of debts. . Length of credit history – 15%; illustrates credit management skills over an extended time. . Credit mix – 10%; shows how you balance different types of credit. . New credit – 10%; indicates your riskiness associated with seeking new credit.

Each of these components is crucial to maintain a good credit score. It's vital to pay your bills on time, keep your debt levels manageable, avoid taking on too much new debt, diversify your credit types and maintain long-standing credit accounts to improve your score.

7.3. Building Good Credit

Building good credit takes time and diligence. Here are some steps you can take to improve your credit:

1. Create and stick to a budget: This will prevent overspending and ensure you have money to cover your bills.

2. Pay your bills on time: Late payments can damage your credit score and transaction history.

3. Keep your credit card and other revolving credit balances low: High outstanding debt can negatively affect your credit score.

4. Apply for and open new credit accounts only as needed: Unnecessary credit can affect your credit score and lead to overextended debt.

5. Pay off debt rather than shifting it around: Also, don't close unused cards as a short-term strategy to improve your credit score.

7.4. Understanding Debt

Debt is money owed by one party to another. It can come in various forms, from consumer debt tied to credit cards to large-scale debts such as mortgages and student loans. Debt may be unavoidable in some cases, but how you manage it can make a significant difference in your overall financial health.

7.5. Types of Debt

There are two primary forms of debt: Secured and Unsecured.

The Secured debt is backed by some form of collateral like a car in the case of an auto loan or a home for a mortgage. If the borrower fails to make timely payments, the lender can confiscate the asset.

On the other hand, Unsecured debt is not tied to any asset, like credit card debt, student loans, or personal loans. While the lender can't directly take any of your assets if you fail to pay, they can take other collection actions.

7.6. Managing Your Debt

Helpful ways to manage and reduce your debts include: . Making a budget: Identify your income channels, necessary expenses, and discretionary spending. Then, allocate a certain portion to pay off your debts. . Prioritizing your debts: Rank them in order of interest rates and focus on paying off the ones with the highest rates first. . Seeking professional assistance: If you feel overwhelmed by your debt, consider enlisting a credit counseling agency's aid. They can help devise a debt management plan for you. . Debt consolidation: You can consider consolidating your debt by transferring high-interest debt to a lower interest account or loan.

Credit and debt indeed serve as a double-edged sword. Utilized properly, they can propel your financial journey forward. However, misuse or lack of understanding can leave you entrapped in financial distress. Thus, acquiring knowledge and developing good monetary habits are of essence in mastering the use of these powerful financial tools.

Chapter 8. Planning for Retirement: A Future-Proof Approach

Planning for retirement might seem daunting, but with a future-proof approach, it can be streamlined. Let's begin by understanding the fundamentals of this endeavor.

8.1. Understanding Retirement Planning

Retirement planning is all about setting a financial goal for the period post your professional life and accumulating sufficient resources to achieve this goal. While the concept is simple, the approach to achieve it hinges on several factors like your current age, desired retirement age, expected lifestyle post-retirement, current savings, and income potential.

A future-proof retirement plan isn't just about saving money. It's about strategically investing across various asset classes such as equity, debt, gold, and real estate, while also ensuring that the plan is flexible enough to calibrate based on economic scenarios and personal situations.

8.2. Factoring in Inflation

One common pitfall in retirement planning is neglecting the role of inflation. Given that retirement is a goal that's usually decades away, inflation significantly erodes the purchasing power of money over time. For instance, a yearly expense of $30,000 now would amount to approximately $80,000 after 30 years, assuming an average inflation rate of 3%.

Therefore, while planning for retirement, the growth rate of investments should ideally be higher than the rate of inflation to maintain the same standard of living post-retirement.

8.3. Assessing Retirement Corpus

Understanding how much money you would need to sustain your lifestyle post-retirement is the first step. You can use a simple formula to calculate the retirement corpus:

Table 1. Retirement Corpus

Current Annual Expenses	$X
Inflation Rate	i%
Expected Retirement Age	Y years
Life Expectancy	Z years
Retirement Corpus	= $X * (1 + i%)^(Y-Z)

Remember that this corpus should provide you a revenue stream that can substitute your income post-retirement and cater to any contingencies.

8.4. Creating a Retirement Portfolio

Creating a retirement portfolio involves diversifying your investments across multiple asset classes. When you are far from retirement, you can afford to take higher risks for better returns. Over time, the risk appetite reduces, and the focus should shift to capital preservation.

A careful mix of equities, debt instruments, real estate, and gold can create a balanced portfolio. Regular rebalancing of the portfolio based on market conditions and future goals helps maintain the risk-return balance.

8.5. Social Security and Employer-Sponsored Plans

For those employed, contributing to social security is a fundamental part of retirement planning. At the same time, taking advantage of employer-sponsored plans, like 401(k), 403(b), or IRAs, can offer benefits like employer matches and tax advantages.

8.6. Healthcare Planning

As you age, healthcare expenses rise. Therefore, healthcare planning is an important aspect of retirement planning. Options like health savings accounts (HSAs) or long-term care insurance can go a long way towards ensuring that hefty medical bills do not derail your retirement plan.

8.7. Estate Planning

It's equally crucial to have a comprehensive estate plan. Drafting a will, setting up trusts, and identifying power of attorney, all fall under this domain. These steps ensure that your assets are distributed as you wish after your demise and reduce potential disputes.

8.8. Regular Review and Adjustments

A future-proof retirement plan is not a 'set and forget' type. It should be regularly reviewed, at least annually, to make adjustments for changes in income, expenses, financial goals, market conditions, and health issues.

Retirement planning may look complicated, but it is an essential part of financial planning. With this future-proof approach, you can navigate your way to a comfortable and sustainable post-retirement life. Remember, the earlier you start, the more comfortable this journey will be.

Chapter 9. Risk Management and Insurance: Securing your Wealth

Risk fundamentally prevails in every aspect of life, and financial planning isn't exempt. Every decision, every investment, and every step towards financial freedom is fraught with certain levels and types of risks. Risk Management, therefore, becomes a pivotal cornerstone of any sound Personal Financial Planning. Ensuring one's wealth against potential pitfalls and vulnerabilities must not be overlooked. This comprehensive guide, therefore, will guide you through understanding the concept of Risk Management and explain how insurance can help secure your wealth.

9.1. Understanding Risk

While the term 'risk' is generally associated with causes of harm or damage, in the financial world, it typically implies volatility, which can be either positive (upward trend) or negative (downward trend). Each financial decision you make will have an associated risk, and learning to manage this is one of the keys to financial success.

Risk can be categorized into two types – systemic and non-systemic risks. Systemic risks affect the entire market, and hence cannot be eliminated. On the other hand, non-systemic risks affect only certain sectors, industries or companies and can be minimized or eliminated through diversification.

9.2. Importance of Risk Management

Although the element of risk can never be eliminated entirely, effective risk management can substantially minimize its potential negative impact. Risk management forms an integral part of the financial planning process, helping you manage uncertainties that might hinder your financial goals.

It's often seen that people focus more on wealth creation and miss the equally significant aspect of wealth protection. The importance of risk management can be surmised from the time-worn adage, "Protect before you invest."

9.3. Basics of Risk Management – Evaluate, Plan, Implement, Review

The process of risk management primarily involves four steps:

1. Identify and analyze the risks

2. Determine the most effective risk management technique

3. Implement the selected techniques

4. Regularly review and revise the plan

During the identification phase, consider all possible risks – be it market-related, health-related, or risks related to loss of property. Next, strategize your reaction against each risk identified and how you can best protect your wealth.

9.4. Understanding Insurance – Safeguarding Your Wealth

One of the most common risk management techniques is insurance. Insurance is essentially a contract in which, in return for premium payments, you transfer the risk of unexpected financial losses to an insurance company. The insurance companies pool the premiums from many insured individuals to pay for the losses that some insured individuals may incur.

The purpose of insurance is not profit but to provide financial stability by reducing monetary losses. Depending on the risk you want to cover, you can choose from various types of insurance such as life insurance, health insurance, property insurance, auto insurance, and more.

9.5. Life Insurance and Wealth Protection

Among the different types of insurance, life insurance is probably the most significant when it comes to wealth protection. It ensures that your dependents are financially secure in the event of your untimely death. Through the emotional turmoil that follows your loss, the financial protection your life insurance offers can help them maintain their standard of living.

Furthermore, life insurance is also an excellent tool for wealth creation. Many life insurance policies offer savings and investment options, giving you opportunities for wealth accumulation.

9.6. Health Insurance – Safeguarding Your Savings

In the face of rising medical costs, a serious illness or hospitalization can make a significant dent in your savings, potentially pushing your financial plans off track. Health insurance becomes essential to avoid such a situation. In return for regular premium payments, a health insurance policy covers medical and surgical expenses, shielding you from potentially enormous financial burdens related to healthcare.

9.7. Property and Auto Insurance

Your home or car is a valuable asset that may have required significant financial investment. Property and auto insurances ensure these assets are protected against the risk of damage or loss due to accidents, theft, or natural disasters.

By routinely paying a lesser premium, you transfer the risk of potential colossal financial losses to the insurance company.

9.8. Making the Right Insurance Decision

Understanding the type of insurance needed can be tricky, and it's recommended to take advice from a financial advisor or insurance consultant to make conscious and careful decisions. Your decision should consider not just the price, but also the coverage, claim settlement ratio, and customer service.

While navigating through the labyrinth of personal finance may seem like an arduous task, the process of risk management, with a focus on insurance, can make the journey significantly less treacherous. It might not eliminate all uncertainties but helps secure your financial future against unforeseen events. With adequate risk management, your hard-earned wealth might not merely survive but prosper in any financial climate.

Chapter 10. Tax Insights: Keeping More of your Money

Every financial journey begins with an understanding of taxes, as they can leave a significant impact on an individual's overall financial scenario. Ignorance or mismanagement of the tax structure and policies can contribute to financial hardships, as you can end up paying more than you need to. It is crucial to understand tax laws, which can help you plan your finances more efficiently and keep more of your earnings. Let's delve deeper into the insights of taxes and how you can use these insights to save more money.

10.1. The Basic Premise of Taxes

Taxes represent the monetary obligations you owe to the government. The revenue obtained is used towards various government projects, which benefit the citizens and the economy of the country. Your income can be taxed in several ways, which might include income tax, property tax, sales tax, and even inheritance tax. Understanding each tax type and how they influence your finances is the first step to keeping more of your money.

10.2. Understand Income Tax

The largest source of tax income for many governments is the income tax, which is applied to earnings received by individuals or businesses. Income tax can be progressive, regressive, or proportional, and the specifics of each are determined by your country's tax law.

Progressive tax systems tax higher income at higher rates. As a result, wealthy individuals have a larger tax liability compared to those with lower incomes. This type of system is common in countries where wealth redistribution is a policy aim.

Regressive tax systems do the opposite. Lower-income individuals are tax at higher rates relative to their income, while wealthier individuals pay a lower percentage of their income in taxes.

In a proportional tax system—or a flat tax system—every taxpayer pays the same percentage of their income in taxes, regardless of how much they earn.

This basic understanding allows you to place your financial planning within the right context.

10.3. Tax Deductions and Credits

Tax deductions and tax credits are incentives provided by the government to motivate specific behavior or to ease the tax burden for certain demographics. A tax deduction reduces your taxable income, while a tax credit directly reduces your tax liability.

Deductions involve certain expenses, which can be subtracted from your taxable income. Examples of these are contributions to retirement accounts, mortgage interest, or tuition fees.

Tax credits directly reduce the amount of tax you owe, dollar for dollar. Examples of these might include child tax credits, earned income tax credit, and education credits.

Knowing which deductions and credits apply to you can drastically reduce your tax bill and allow you to keep more of your money.

10.4. Proper Record Keeping

Efficiently maintained tax records can be your strongest ally when it comes to tax payments. Receipts, bank statements, pay slips, and reports of any kind of income are indispensable for the tax filing process. Efficient record-keeping also ensures that you claim all the eligible tax deductions and credits.

10.5. Working with Tax Professionals

A tax professional can provide valuable insights into your unique tax situation, informing you of strategies and policies that can minimize your tax liability. They can help you better understand the regulations, and keep you apprised of any changes in the tax laws. They can also assist with dispute resolution with tax authorities if any issue arises.

10.6. Plan for Taxes in Advance

To keep more of your money, it's essential to plan for taxes throughout the year, not just during tax season. By making adjustments to your finances in advance, you can leverage tax laws to reduce your overall liability.

10.7. Summing Up

No financial journey is complete without an in-depth understanding of the tax landscapes that shape it. Tax planning should go hand-in-hand with your other financial strategies and goals. Remember, nothing in the realm of taxes is 'one size fits all.' Always examine how newly enacted tax laws impact your specific circumstances, and never shy away from seeking professional assistance when needed. Armed with this knowledge, you can confidently keep more of your hard-earned money, and set yourself up for greater financial prosperity.

Chapter 11. Etching the Path to Financial Freedom: Strategies for the Long Run

Unbeknownst to most, the journey to financial freedom is less about the destination and more about the path you tread. The cornerstone of this path is being conscious of your financial decisions, planning, and taking control of your money instead of it controlling you. Exceptional strategies can guide one towards abundant economic success and independence, regardless of how winding the trail may seem. This chapter builds the foundations of those strategies that could adapt, withstand economic climate fluctuation, and persist into the long run.

11.1. Understanding Your Financial Picture

To embark on this journey, you first need a clear understanding of your financial picture. Create a personal balance sheet that outlines your assets (what you own) and liabilities (what you owe). This balance sheet acts as a fiscal mirror, reflecting your financial health. It is essential to update this regularly, as your financial position may change over time.

In parallel, track and categorize your expenses. Being conscious of spending habits enables the detection and reduction of discretionary and incidental costs. Several personal finance applications can automate this tracking, thereby making it easier to understand how your money flows, contributing to a comprehensive financial picture.

11.2. Establishing a Foundation: Emergency Fund

'Rainy days' are inevitable. Before moving towards growth, it's imperative to create a security net, your Emergency Fund. This reserve protects you during unexpected circumstances such as job loss, medical emergencies, or major home repairs. As a guideline, you should strive to save a minimum of three to six months' worth of living expenses. This fund should be readily accessible (like in a high-yield savings account) yet separate from your daily transactional account to avoid unintentional usage.

11.3. Defining Your Financial Goals

After understanding your financial state and creating a security net, the next step is to define your financial goals. Be it saving for a home, planning for retirement, clearing debt, creating a college fund for your children, or a desire for wealth accumulation, every individual's financial goals are unique.

Treat these goals as a financial roadmap. Notably, these goals should be SMART - Specific, Measurable, Attainable, Relevant, and Time-based. Define what you want to achieve, the amount needed, how long it will take, and finally, formulate a plan to attain these goals.

11.4. The Power of Budgeting

A well-structured budget is your financial blueprint. It gives purpose to every penny earned. Align your budget with your financial goals; allocate funds towards essential expenses, savings, investments, and debt reduction. This step is particularly important as segregating your income towards definite expenditure categories avoids wasteful spending.

Budgeting strategies vary from person to person. Some popular methods include the 50/20/30 rule (essentials/savings/flex spending), zero-based budgeting (every dollar has a job), or envelope budgeting. Choose a method that fits your lifestyle, goals, and helps you maintain financial discipline.

11.5. Clearing the Debt Hurdles

Debt can be a significant hindrance to financial freedom. Prioritize clearing off high-interest debts like credit cards over low-interest ones like student loans. Consider strategies such as the snowball method (paying off smallest debts first to garner momentum) or the avalanche method (prioritizing highest interest debts). Debt reduction increases your disposable income, which can be channelled towards your financial goals.

11.6. Igniting Growth: Investing

Money left idle loses value due to inflation. To ensure your money works for you, consider investing. The power of compound interest, famously termed the 'Eighth Wonder of the World,' transforms small, consistent investments into significant wealth over the long term.

Diversification is key. Invest across different asset types – stocks, bonds, real estate – to maximize return and limit risk. Maintain a balanced portfolio that corresponds with your risk tolerance, investment horizon, and financial goals.

11.7. Retirement Planning: Supercharging your Future

Retirement planning should be your ultimate financial goal. Make use of tax-advantaged retirement accounts like 401(k), Roth IRA or traditional IRA. Regular, disciplined contributions towards these accounts, thanks to the magic of compound interest, can accumulate substantial wealth, ensuring a comfortable retirement.

Furthermore, evaluating and purchasing appropriate insurance (health, life, auto, home, etc.) shields you and your family during unforeseen circumstances, and safeguards your wealth and retirement savings.

The path towards financial freedom isn't a single well-defined road. It's an amalgamation of understanding, discipline, and strategic choices that align with your personal financial landscape. It's never too late to start on this road. Armed with these strategies, your path would not only be etched but also illuminated. After all, the journey to financial freedom is yours to charter—a journey where the real treasure is the peace of mind that stems from financial security and independence.